Dinosa
of the Triassic Period

Dinosaurs Edition

Explore Series ©

James Willoughby

Copyright © 2019 Explore Series Books. All rights reserved. http://exploreseries.com

No part of this book may be reproduced by any means whatever without prior written permission of the copyright holder, except brief portions quoted for the purpose of review. We do protect our copyright by all legal means.

The information in this book has been carefully researched and checked for factual correctness. However, the information contained in this book is for general information and entertainment purposes only, and the publisher assumes no responsibility for unintentional errors or omissions.

All images in this book have either been purchased or are reproduced with permission or attribution by the original copyright holder.

ISBN: 978-1097901531

If you need to contact us, you can do so via our website below. You can also see all of the other **Dinosaur** books and Kindle eBooks I have available here:

http://exploreseries.com

Dedication

To all the curious children!

TABLE OF CONTENTS

About the Triassic Period 1
Daemonosaurus 2
Chindesaurus 3
Gojirasaurus 4
Coelophysis 5
Tawa Hallae 6
Agnosphitys 8
Antetonitrus 9
Asilisaurus 10
Eodromaeus 12
Alwalkeria 13
Efraasia 14
Eocursor 15
Panphagia 16
Liliensternus 17
Pisanosaurus 18
Eoraptor 19
Zupaysaurus 21
Riojasaurus 22
Euskelosaurus 23
Herrerasaurus 24
Melanorosaurus 25
Sanjuansaurus 26
Unaysaurus 27
Thecodontosaurus 30
Staurikosaurus 32
Pampadromaeus 33

Shuvosaurus 34
Sellosaurus 35
Pantydraco 36
Lophostropheus 37
Camposaurus 38
Dictionary 42
Reference 43

AUTHOR'S NOTES

When I use initials, it indicates which continent or country where that Dino was living (US=United States, SA=South America, EU=Europe, AF=Africa).

Each Dinosaur image gives the name of the Dinosaur as well as its meaning, if known, and a little bit about them.

There are four possible descriptions of these Dino diets.

> **Herbivore** = vegetarian / plant eater
> **Carnivore** = meat eater
> **Omnivore** = plant and meat eater
> **Insectivore** = bugs and very small animals

I have also included a **Dictionary (D)** to explain some words you may not be familiar with. . Once a word is explained in the Dictionary, I did not include the (D) after its name again.

There is also a **Reference (R)** section if you would like to do some more research. Make sure to type the exact website address on one line to insure that you have the right one.

Sometimes Dinosaurs are called "Dino" as a nickname or short version of their "official" name.

All weights are in pounds and length in feet and inches. If you'd like to convert those to metrics, you can find a handy conversion application here online (make sure you type the entire link on one line in your browser):

http://www.metric-conversions.org/

The pronunciations given are the most common way to say it in U.S. English.

v

About the Triassic Period

The Triassic Period for Dinosaurs was from about 251 to 199 million years ago. All the Dinosaurs in this book are from that time.

The chart below shows that the Triassic Period is the oldest one.

Many of the animals from the Triassic Period are considered prehistoric reptiles, issuing in the first "age of the Dinosaur." Since the lines are so blurry between the two, I am including them all under the broad Dinosaurs category.

We hope you have fun looking at these pictures and learning a little something about these Dinosaurs from the Triassic period.

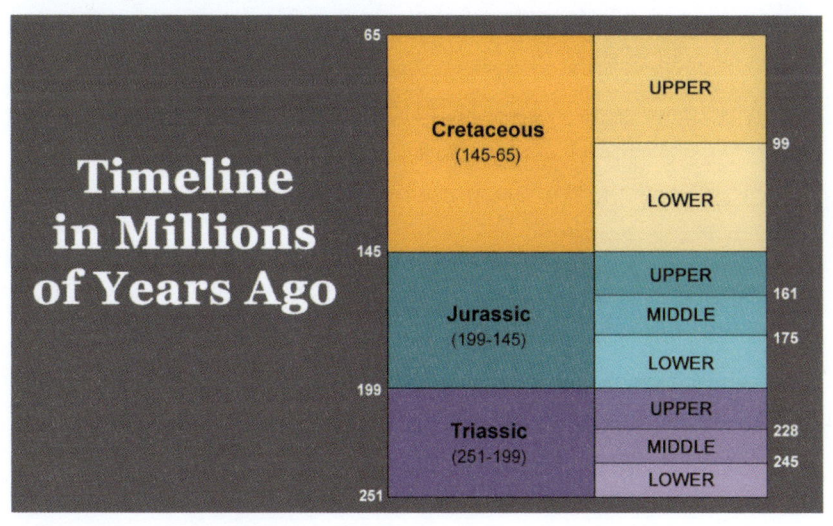

Timeline in Millions of Years Ago			
65			
	Cretaceous (145-65)	UPPER	99
		LOWER	
145		UPPER	161
	Jurassic (199-145)	MIDDLE	175
		LOWER	
199		UPPER	228
	Triassic (251-199)	MIDDLE	245
251		LOWER	

Now, let's get started!

Daemonosaurus
"Demon Reptile"
(day-mow-no-sore-us)

About the size of a large dog, this recently discovered Dinosaur had huge eyes, walked on its back legs and was a carnivore (D). Its fossil was discovered in New Mexico (US) in an area that is well known for finding fossil remains. The Daemonosaurus is a distant relative of the Tyrannosaurus Rex, which lived in the upper Cretaceous Period.

Chindesaurus
"Lizard from Chinde Point"
(chin-de-sore-us)

The world "chinde" means "evil spirit" in the Navajo language. It was first discovered in Arizona (US) and was named when they found a partial skeleton. As of this writing, five incomplete skeletons have been found.

Gojirasaurus
"Godzilla Lizard"
(go-jee-ruh-sore-us)

Gojira is the Japanese word for Godzilla, the fictional monster from the 1954 original movie. Paleontologists (D) are guessing quite a bit about this Dino because they only have a partial skeleton – which was discovered in New Mexico. They have estimated that it was about 18' long and weighed between 300 and 400 pounds.

Coelophysis
"Hollow Form"
(see-lo-fi-sis)

This Dino was given that nickname because its limb bones were hollow inside. It walked on its hind legs and was probably a fast runner. Scientists were lucky with Coelophysis because they have found several complete skeletons of this carnivore (especially in New Mexico, US), so they can easily see what it looked like. It had tough skin, a long tail, flexible neck and lethal teeth.

Tawa Hallae
"Sun God Hall"
(tah-wuh hall-ee)

Named after the Pueblo Indian Sun God, the Tawa is a type of Theropoda (D). This Dino was named for Ruth Hall, founder of the Ghost Ranch Museum of Paleontology (R) Quite a few skeletal remains have been found in the Hayden Quarry in New Mexico (US), allowing the scientists to estimate an adult was between 6' and 8' long. The juvenile fossils were estimated to be about 30% smaller than that.

Estimated sizes of a Tawa Hallae juvenile and adult compared to a human being.

This is what the artist had determined that a Tawa might have looked like, based on fossil evidence. I don't know who that little guy with him is supposed to be!

Agnosphitys
"Unknown Begetter"
(ag-nose,fi,tees)

They have only found one species of this Dinosaur, consisting of a partial skeleton (found back in 2002), so there is a lot of disagreement about it. A "begetter" usually refers to the father of something, so I guess some scientists believe this to be one of the original Dinos. But some others believe it wasn't even a Dinosaur. Wonder if we'll ever know for sure...

Antetonitrus
"Before the Thunder"
(anti-tone-e-truss)

The Antetonitrus was a quadrupedal herbivore, meaning that it walked on all four feet and was a plant eating Dino. It was believed to be recovered from a land which was part of the Triassic Period but that was later disputed as studies indicated it was more like recovered from the Early Jurassic Upper Elliot Formation in South Africa. So, maybe I should move this over to the Jurassic edition of tis series!

Antetonitrus was a big guy, estimated to be about 33' long, weighing as much as 2 tons. There is some speculation that it could still use its front two feet for grabbing things.

Asilisaurus
"Ancestor Lizard"
(ah-see-lee-sore-us)

This Dinosaur was about the same size as a Labrador Retriever dog. The scientists say that the discovery of this Dino in Tanzania meant that there were Dinosaurs 10 million years earlier than was thought!

Parts of about 12 skeletons were found in 2007. Since none of them were whole, the scientists had to piece together a skeleton by combining bones from all of them.

Unlike most of its fellow Dinosaurs from that time period, the Asilisaurus ran on all four feet. It had very skinny legs, teeth that looked like pegs and a beak-like jaw.

The image on the next page shows the Asilisaurus with a sail-backed Poposauroid in the background.

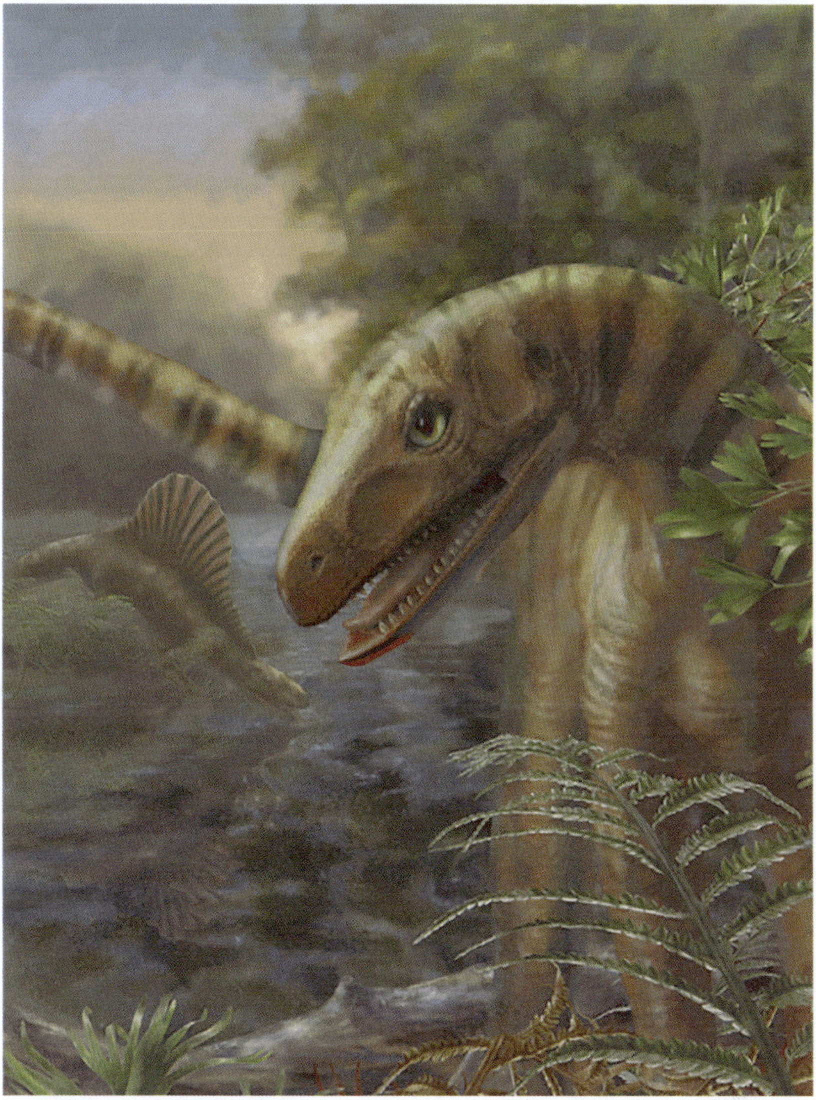

Eodromaeus
"Dawn Runner"
(ee-oh-drom-ee-us)

Eodromaeus wasn't very large, measuring only about 4' long and weighing less than 15 pounds, with a long neck and tail. This meat-eating Dino was first announced to the world in 2011, and may be the earliest known relative of the T-Rex. Paleontologists pieced together two skeletons from the Ischigualasto-Villa Unión Basin in northwestern Argentina to make one almost complete specimen.

Alwalkeria
"For Alick Walker:
(al-wah-care-ee-yuh)

This Dinosaur was bipedal (D) Dinosaur that lived in India during the Late Triassic Period. It got its name in 1994 after it was discovered that its original name (Walkeria maleriensis) had already been used to name a sea creature. Its new name was to honor Alick Donald Walker, a famous British paleontologist. Due to its oddly shaped teeth, it was difficult to tell what its diet was, so it was determined that is must be an omnivore (D).

Efraasia
"E. Fraas"
(ee-frah-zee-uh)

Named after Eberhard Fraas, the man who discovered it in Germany. Efraasia walked on all four feet and was known to be a plant eater. This Dino was been mislabeled four times. By 1984 the fossils were mistakenly thought to be portions of a young Sellosaurus, but eighteen years later, were finally identified as a separate genus.

Eocursor
"Dawn Runner"
(ee-oh-kur-sur)

This Dinosaur seems to be at the very beginning of Ornithischian (D) Dinosaurs. These include Dinosaurs like Stegosaurus and Triceratops. Although fossils of the Eocursor were first discovered in 1993 in South Africa, they weren't "officially" named until 2007. There is some dispute as to whether this was a "Late Triassic" or an "Early Jurassic" Dino. This guy is not very big at only about three feet long and two pounds, just a little larger than a Fox.

Panphagia
"All to Eat"

From the Middle Triassic period, this bipedal Dino was most likely an omnivore from what the scientists can determine. He wasn't that big (about 6' long), but had a very long tail in comparison to his size. They are surmising that this was a "transitional" Dino because it had characteristics in common with both earlier Dinos and Dinosaurs that evolved after Panphagia existed.

Liliensternus
"Lilienstern's One"
(lil-ee-uhn-stir-nus)

He got his unusual name and nickname because he was named after Dr. Hugo Rühle von Lilienstern, a German paleontologist. Liliensternus was one of the largest carnivores of its time, measuring about 15' long and weighing in at a fierce 200 pounds! It has five fingers, two of which are smaller than the rest, and a long tail which helped it stay balanced on its two, strong back legs.

Pisanosaurus
"Pisano lizard"
(piss-ah-no-sore-us)

This small Dinosaur (probably 3.3 feet long and 15 pounds) seems to be at the root of Ornithischian evolution. This one sure looks like a bird! It is named in honor of Argentine paleontologist Juan Arnaldo Pisano Scientists are not certain whether this Dino deserves its own classification because there are so few fossil specimens available to study. In fact, the only skeleton discovered (in Argentina) was incomplete, lacking several key bones needed to absolutely identify the whole. They *believe* it had a long tail, but since no tail has been found, it is just a guess on their part.

Eoraptor
"Dawn Thief or Plunderer"
(ee-oh-rap-tor)

This Dinosaur has many features that are typical of a raptor such as being bipedal and having sharp teeth. Fortunately, there are several skeletons of this Dino, all well preserved, so scientists know that this one of the earliest known Dinosaurs.

Here is how big the Eoraptor was compared to a human being.

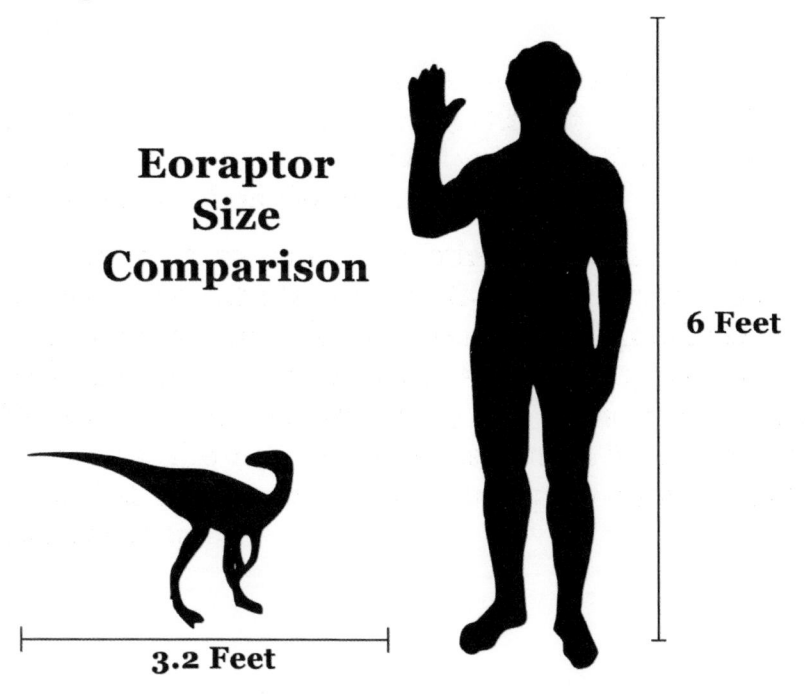

Eoraptor Size Comparison

6 Feet

3.2 Feet

Eoraptor

Zupaysaurus
"Devil Lizard"
(zoo-pay-sore-us)

This Dinosaur lived during the late Triassic Period to early Jurassic Period (D) in Argentina. Although a full skeleton hasn't yet been discovered, scientists have determined that Zupaysaurus walked on two feet and had parallel crests running along the top of its nose. This was based on a possible Dilophosaurid (D) trace fossil. Scientists believe it was about 13 feet long, although there is some dispute about this.

Riojasaurus
"La Rioja lizard"
(ree-oh-hah-sore-us)

This was a *huge* Dinosaur from the late Triassic Period. It was named after La Rioja Province in Argentina where it was found. He was about 35' long, weighed nearly a ton and was an herbivore (D). He was big and bulky and his legs were massive –but its backbones were hallow, which made the load a little lighter for those big legs to carry.

Euskelosaurus
"Good-Leg Lizard"
(you-skell-uh-sore-us)

Euskelosaurus was also a *huge* Dinosaur, bigger even than Riojasaurus. He was 40 feet long and about 2 tons and was believed to live in South Africa and Lesotho. It got its own classification in 1866 when a spine and a limb were found, but in 1902 was given its present name.

Some scientists believe it is the same as another Dinosaur called Plateosaurus, which was renamed Euskelosaurus in 1976. Controversy and different opinions still exist as to whether they are the same animal.

Herrerasaurus
"Herrera's lizard"
(her-rare-uh-sore-us)

Herrerasaurus was one of the very first Dinosaurs to walk the planet. This Dinosaur was named in honor of a rancher, Victorino Herrera, who first discovered a fossil of Herrerasaurus. Although this was not a complete skeleton, but when a complete skill was found in 1988, they were able to complete reconstruct this Dino. It wasn't a very large animal, standing only about 3.5' at its hipbone, but it was a vicious carnivore anyway. It had a very unusual skull, with 10 holes in it – two for the nose and two for the eyes, plus another six which probably made the head less heavy.

Melanorosaurus
"Black Mountain Lizard"
(mel-uh-nor-uh-sore-us)

This is another very big Dinosaur, about 35' long and weighing between two and three tons. It was an herbivore, as many of the large Dinos were. Like Riojasaurus, this Dino has large, thick legs, and is probably a close relative of it as well. It is believed to be the largest land animal of its time.

Sanjuansaurus
"San Juan Province Lizard"
(san-whan-sore-us)

The information on this Dino is based on a partial skeleton found in Argentina, which seems to be a real treasure trove of valuable Dinosaur fossils. Based on only that small specimen, it has been determined that this was a small (5', 50 pound) carnivore that walked on two legs. They have concluded that it was closely related to both the Eoraptor and especially the Herrerasaurus. They both had similar skulls, neck vertebrae, back vertebrae, hip vertebrae, scapulas, and hip bones.

Unaysaurus
"Black Water lizard"
(oon-aye-sore-us)

This is one of the oldest Dinosaurs ever found. It was discovered in Southern Brazil in 1998.

The fossils of Unaysaurus were so well preserved that some of the bones were still connected to each other! This made it easier to determine certain things about their anatomy, like their size. Unaysaurus was fairly small (2-3 feet) and light (about 150 pounds) and walked on two feet. It was also an herbivore.

Some of the oldest Dinosaurs in history have been found in Brazil. Unaysaurus was related, believe it or not, to some of the largest animals to ever walk the Earth, like the Brachiosaurus from the Jurassic Period.

Because it is so similar to other Dinosaurs found in Germany the experts surmise that the Unaysaurus was able to travel across the large land mass that existed way back then from Europe to South America. It was known as Pangaea (D) and included every one of the present–day continents. The discovery of Unaysaurus in Brazil seems to show that it was easy for different types of Dinosaurs to make this trip.

Unaysaurus

Pangaea

About 300 million year ago there was one "super continent" called Pangaea. About 100 million years after that the continents started to split and divide into the Earth as we now know it (Europe, North America, Africa, etc.) This is what Earth looked like before the land mass started drifting apart to form the different continents.

Thecodontosaurus
"Socket-Toothed Lizard" or Bristol Dinosaur
(theek-uh-don-tuh-sore-us)

This was one of the first Dinosaurs from the Triassic Period ever discovered. It got its name because its teeth were not fused with the jaw bone as with many other Dinosaurs, but rather were each in separate tooth holes. It was an herbivore with a long, narrow head, had a body that measured about 6.5 feet long, and is one of very few Dinosaurs that lived exclusively in the present day United Kingdom. The bones of a Thecodontosaurus were found near Bristol during the 1970s.

CAUTION

Although the following image is of a carnivore, it is extremely gruesome and probably not appropriate for very young children. Young boys, however, will no doubt love it.

It is a drawing of a Staurikosaurus dining on a Dicynodont (D).

In any case, you may choose to skip over the following page if you are concerned.

Staurikosaurus
"Southern Cross Lizard"
(stoh-rick-uh-sore-us)

This Dinosaur is from the Late Triassic Period in Brazil. It was about 6' long and 75 pounds, but it was a serious carnivore. It has slender legs and arms and five digits on each foot, and it was a quick runner and very agile. The nickname refers to the star formation of the same name. Not too many fossils have been found of this Dino, possibly because it may have lived in forested areas, where skeletal remains are rarely found.

This one is having dinner. Ew.

Pampadromaeus
"Plains runner"
(pom-pa-dro-may-us)

This Dinosaur is only known from part of one well preserved skeleton found in Southern Brazil. It had long back legs and a narrow nose. It had unusual teeth that were shaped like leaves in the front, but curved ones in the back – which have led scientists to conclude that it was an omnivore.

Shuvosaurus
"Shuvo Lizard"
(shoe-voe-sore-us)

This Dinosaur is from the late Triassic Period but wasn't discovered until 1993. It is named after the son (Shuvo) of Sankar Chatterjee, the paleontologist who discovered it in Texas (US).

This Dinosaur was about 10' long and weighed about 100 pounds.

As you can see in the picture below, it had a beak-shaped head...but it has no teeth. That didn't stop it from being a meat-eater however. Think of a modern-day hawk. Their beaks are easily capable of tearing into meat.

Sellosaurus
"Saddle Lizard"
(sell-oh-sore-us)

Although he was only about 7' long, Sellosaurus weighed in at close to 500 pounds! He had five fingers on his hands and a long thumb claw. Sellosaurus skeletons have been discovered in Nordwurttemberg, West Germany

This Dino is one of the more well-documented ones with over 20 partial skeletons found so far. Still, there is disagreement as to what to call it -- most paleontologists think it should be classified as a Plateosaurus (D). The two Dinos are very similar in many ways, and Sellosaurus was most likely an ancestor of the Plateosaurus. But Sellosaurur fossils are rare and Plateosaurus fossils are found in abundance.

Pantydraco
"Pant-y-ffynnon Dragon"
(pan-tee-dray-co)

This unusually named Dinosaur got that name from the region in South Wales where it was found. Not much is known about it since the findings are based the partial remains of one juvenile. They believe it was small (6' and 100 pounds), bipedal and an omnivore – but hard to know for sure with such small evidence.

Lophostropheus
"Crested Vertebrae"
(low-foe-strow-fee-us)

A partial skeleton of this Dinosaur was discovered in France in 1966. It was preserved in rock, which was very unusual for that time frame (Triassic into Jurassic Period) because that was a transitional time in Dinosaur history and it's not very well documented yet.

Lophostropheus had an interesting crest on its head and was around 17' long. This carnivore walked on its hind legs and had the typical shorter forearms.

Camposaurus
"Charles Lewis Camp's Lizard"
(camp-oh-sore-us)

This is a small carnivore Dino. Because so few fossils have been found (partial lower leg bones), it is hard to estimate its exact size. The specimen that *was* discovered was in the Placerias quarry of the Bluewater Creek Formation in northeastern Arizona (US).

Its name is often confused with another Dinosaur called the Camptosaurus, but they are entirely different and are even from different Periods (the Camptosaurus is from the Jurassic Period).

This artist's drawing is pretty much a guess based on its relatives.

A little something extra…

Here are a few more Dinosaurs from the Triassic Period for which I couldn't find any images. Since it was so long ago, the fossil evidence was harder to find and many times scientists couldn't determine exactly what they looked like.

Agrosaurus
"Field Lizard"
(ag-roe-sore-us)

This Dino got its name because the original remains where originally found in a field, first thought to be in Australia, and later thought to be from England. Apparently the fossils were brought to England aboard a British ship, but the ship's log did not record it. So, there has been much confusion about its origins since 1891.

Caseosaurus
"E. C. Case's lizard"
(kay-zee-oh-sore-us)

Also a North American Dinosaur from the late Triassic era. It was found in Texas and some have guessed that it may be misidentified – that it is really a Chindesaurus.

Chromogisaurus
"Painted Valley"
(krome-oh-jeh-sore-us)

Only a single specimen has been found so far of this Dino. The bones were located in Argentina and included a partial skeleton with no skull, parts of the front and back legs, the pelvis and two tail bones from the spine.

[Authors Note] There are many more Dinosaurs from the Triassic Period that have little known about them. Check the Reference section below to learn more about those that have never been given formally published scientific names.

Thanks very much for picking up a copy of "Dinosaurs of the Triassic Period"

I hope you enjoyed it and learned a little something along the way.

I have written many books for the Explore Series Publishers, many on wild animals like Tigers, Rhinos and Lions, and I strive to make sure each one is fun and informative.

I could not have done this on my own and the help I received from the Explore Series team of researchers and editors is very much appreciated!

Thanks!

Jim

Customer Reviews of a few of our Wild Animals Edition Books!

★★★★★ A Barrel Full of Monkeys and Fun!
By **Emma Stone**
Amazon Verified Purchase
This Review is from: Monkeys & Apes (Explore Series) Kindle Edition .
This is a great book filled with beautiful photos and information about monkeys and gorillas. My son and I loved the closeup photos of the monkeys and gorillas and enjoyed the wide variety shown in the book. This is a great book for parents and children to read and enjoy together!

★★★★★ Amazing!
By **Sierra**
Amazon Verified Purchase
This review is from: Elephants (Explore Series) Kindle Edition
This book was amazing. I'm 12 years old and I'm doing a book report about elephants and this book uses cute pictures of elephants and their stuff!!!!!!!! Love it.

★★★★★ Dinosaurs, Dinosaurs, Dinosaurs!
By **John Marks**
Amazon Verified Purchase
This veview is from: Dinosaurs 4-Pack (Explore Series) Kindle Edition
Wow! My son loves this and it's a great item to have in the car!!!!

Dictionary

Bipedal: A Dinosaur that walks on two legs.

Carnivore: A meat eater.

Chindesaurus: A Dinosaur that lived during the latter part of the Triassic Period. It was a small, bipedal Dinosaur.

Dicynodont: Herbivorous animal.

Dilophosauridae: The name comes from the distinctive two crests on the head. (A crest is a comb or tuft of feathers, fur, or skin on the head.)

Fossils: The remains or impression of a Dinosaur preserved in petrified form or as a mold in rock.

Herbivore: A Dinosaur adapted to eating plant materials, like foliage or marine algae, as the main part of its diet.

Jurassic Period: 201.3–145 million years ago

Omnivore: A Dinosaur that eats both plants and animals.

Ornithischian: Plant eaters with bird-like hips.

Paleontologist: A scientist who studies fossils.

Pangaea: Pronounced *pan-gee-uh*. An extremely large area of land which existed millions of years ago, made up of <u>all</u> the present continents.

Plateosaurus: moderate-sized chiefly bipedal Triassic saurischian dinosaurs

Therapoda: A Dinosaur that is characterized by hollow bones and three-toed limbs.

Reference

Ghost Ranch Museum of Paleontology

https://www.ghostranch.org/explore/museums/museum-of-paleontology/

About the Eodromaeus

https://www.youtube.com/watch?v=S9UlA7ZG6u4

The Princeton Field Guide to Dinosaurs

https://amzn.to/3o2wgXv

BBC – Early, Deep Roots of the Eocursor

http://news.bbc.co.uk/2/hi/science/nature/6744955.stm

List of informally named Dinosaurs
This list includes Dinosaurs from the Triassic, Cretaceous and Jurassic Periods.

https://en.wikipedia.org/wiki/List_of_informally_named_dinosaurs

Did you know there are more books in this series in the Amazon store? Check them out for a sneak peek "Look Inside."

BIRD DINOSAURS

Dinosaurs Edition

An EXPLORE SERIES Book

https://exploreseries.com/BirdDinosaurs

DINOSAURS
of the Cretaceous Period

Dinosaurs Edition

An EXPLORE SERIES Book

http://exploreseries.com/dinocretaceous

DINOSAURS
of the Jurassic Period

Dinosaurs Edition

An EXPLORE SERIES Book

http://exploreseries.com/jurassic

There are many more books and eBooks in the "Dinosaur" editions from *Explore Series Publishing*.

Check them out here!

http://exploreseries.com/

Photo Credits:

Due to the lack of actual photographs of Dinosaurs (duh!), we have relied on some of the most respected Dinosaur artists online. We have given appropriate credit and, where known, links to their websites below.

Cover illustration by: Nobumichi Tamura
http://spinops.blogspot.com

Daemonosaurus: Jeff Martz

Asilisaurus: Nobumichi Tamura

Gojirasaurus :Kazimierz Mendlik

Coelophysis: dkfindout.com

Tawa Hallae: Conty (Wikipedia)

Agnosphitys: Karkemish (Wikipedia)

Antetonitrus: PaleoEquii
(https://commons.wikimedia.org/wiki/User:PaleoEquii)

Asilisaurus: M.H.Donnelly

Eodromaeus: Masato Hattori
(http://masahatt02.p2.bindsite.jp/index.html)

Alwalkeria: Karkemish
(https://www.deviantart.com/karkemish00/gallery/)

Efraasia: http://dinosaurpictures.org/Efraasia-pictures

Eocursor: Nobumichi Tamura

Panphagia: Nobumichi Tamura

Pisanosaurus: FunkMonk (Wikipedia)

Eoraptor: Nobumichi Tamura

Eoraptor Size Image: Marmelad (https://commons.wikimedia.org/wiki/User:Marmelad)

Zupaysaurus: FunkMonk (Wikipedia) and http://dinosaurpictures.org

Riojasaurus: (ayay.co.uk/background/dinosaurs/herbivore/riojasaurus-2)

Euskelosaurus: (dinosaurfact.net)

Herrerasaurus: BBC Earth (https://www.bbcearth.com/walking-with-dinosaurs/modal/herrerasaurus/)

Melanorosaurus: Steveoc 86 (https://commons.wikimedia.org/wiki/User:Steveoc_86)

Sanjuansaurus: Nobumichi Tamura

Pangaea map: (https://imgur.com/)

Unaysaurus: Masato Hattori

Thecodontosaurus: (bbc.co.uk)

Staurikosaurus: Nobumichi Tamura

Pampadromaeus: Rodolfo Guaibasaurus (http://www.dinosdobrasil.com.br/index-en.html)

Shuvosaurus: Nobumichi Tamura

Sellosaurus: Nobumichi Tamura

Pantydraco: Nobumichi Tamura

Tomosaurus (www.deviantart.com/tomozaurus)

Printed in Great Britain
by Amazon